PEPSI
THE PROBLEM PUPPY

By **Sandi Parsons**

with illustrations by
Aśka
and helpful advice from
Pepsi Parsons, Canine Story Advisor

Faraway Nearby Ink

Faraway Nearby Ink
PO Box 89
Bassendean WA 6934

Text © Sandi Parsons 2017
www.sandiwrites.com.au
Illustrations & Cover Design © Aśka 2017
www.askaillustration.com
Cover Font & Chapter Headings 'Grandstander Clean' © Tyler Finick
www.tylerfinck.com
Canine Story Advice provided by Pepsi Parsons
www.pepsiparsons.com.au

This is a work of fiction. Names, characters, places, and incidents are either the products of the author's imagination or are used fictitiously. Any resemblance to actual persons, living or dead, businesses, companies, events, or locales is entirely coincidental—with the exception of Pepsi Parsons, who would like the reader to know that although she is a real dog, her shenanigans may have been slightly exaggerated in this book.

All rights reserved. This book or parts thereof may not be reproduced in any form, stored in any retrieval system, or transmitted in any form by any means—electronic, mechanical, photocopy, recording, or otherwise—without prior written permission of the publisher, except as allowed under the Australian Copyright Act 1968.

This book may not be circulated in any form of binding or cover other than in which it was published.

First published by Faraway Nearby Ink in 2017

A Cataloguing-in-Publication entry is available from the National Library of Australia.
ISBN 978-0-9876157-0-1

PEPSI
THE PROBLEM
PUPPY

1.
Pepsi

JACOB RAN INTO my bedroom and poked me. "Wake up, Rosie Posie." He giggled and ran away. He knows he's not allowed in my bedroom.

Last week I put a sign up that said, 'No little brothers allowed. No exceptions. That means you, Jacob!!!!'

Jacob ignored it. I'd spent two hours making a sign with extra special fancy lettering and had forgotten he can't read.

I put my Smurf slippers on and stomped to the kitchen for breakfast. Dad was reading the paper.

"Who sent Jacob into my room?" I glared at Dad.

He grinned back. "Rosie, does that offer to weed the garden still stand? A month, didn't you say?"

I poured milk onto my Weet-Bix. "For a puppy, Dad. Not just because." Jobs on the weekend are as bad as homework.

Dad shrugged. "If you do your jobs now, you might have more time to play with Pepsi."

"Dave!" Mum swatted him with a tea towel.

"We decided not to tell Rosie until you've taken a look at that dog."

"Pepsi?" My heart started to race a little. I've wanted a puppy forever.

"It might be nice for Gran to have some company during the day." Dad winked at me. "In case she gets lonely."

I nodded, holding my breath.

Mum turned to me. "It's not easy to toilet train puppies, and Gran's not steady on her feet. That rules out a puppy. Your dad's done some research."

Dad gave me one of his big silly grins. "So we decided—"

"By 'we' your dad means he talked me around," Mum interrupted.

Dad laughed and continued, "—to choose a dog from the pet shelter. This morning I found a lovely young blue heeler called Pepsi. She's about eight months old."

Mum pushed some bread into the toaster and turned back to me. "According to your dad, blue heelers are smart."

Dad nodded. "I've done my research. Blue heelers are working dogs, smart and quick to learn. Best of all, they're not that big."

I squealed and hugged Mum and then Dad. "When can we get her?" I couldn't stop jumping up and down.

"This isn't a done deal, Rosie," Mum warned. "Dad still has to go and have a look at Pepsi and make sure she's suitable."

I already knew Pepsi would be perfect. Her name was a sign. Our last name is Parsons, and when you put them together, Pepsi Parsons sounded right.

"Please, please let me come too," I begged.

Dad ruffled my hair. "Too much fuss to take Jacob's car seat out."

I knew that wasn't the real reason because when Dad was getting ready I heard Mum say, "I wish you hadn't told her, Dave. She can't go with you to the shelter. If that dog's not suitable, she'll find a way to talk you into bringing her home."

So, I waited on the veranda with my fingers

crossed. When Dad's car pulled into the drive, I saw a flash of bluish grey moving in the back seat.

Dad opened his door and Pepsi jumped over his lap and out of the car. Pepsi didn't look like pictures I've seen of blue heelers.

No black eye patches, just the same mottled blue-grey all over her face. She had some funny little orange patches that looked a bit like eyebrows. Her legs had the same orange markings too, which kind of looked like little puppy socks.

She ran straight to the flower bed at the front of the house and started digging. I snatched up her leash and tugged to try to get her to stop.

She ignored me and dirt flew backwards.

Dad helped me haul Pepsi out of the garden. Little sweat beads ran across his face and he dabbed them with his hanky.

"You wipe her feet off, Rosie. I'll take care of this before your Mum sees it. Don't want to start off on the wrong foot. Your mum loves her garden."

Dad hastily scraped the dirt off the path and back into the garden while I brushed Pepsi's feet. "There," he said. "No harm, no foul."

Mum opened the front door. "Any problems?"

"Nope, nothing to see here."

I rolled my eyes. Dad always says that when he's fixed something he doesn't want Mum to see.

Mum shook her head at him. "Pepsi looks bigger than I expected," she said.

Pepsi's ears pricked up and she bounced onto the veranda towards Mum, pulling me with her.

Dad nodded. "Hmm, yes, about that. Apparently, you can't trust everything you read on the internet. She has big feet and may not have finished growing yet."

Mum gave Dad one of her 'I see' looks. Her nostrils flared and she raised both eyebrows.

She held the door open a little wider so we could come inside.

Jacob yelled, "Pepsi Parsons!" from the kitchen.

Pepsi bowled through the door so fast she nearly knocked Mum over. Mum took a step back to stay on her feet. I made one last lunge forward before the leash pulled out of my hands and Pepsi disappeared into the kitchen.

2.
An Unwanted Present

MUM FROWNED AND gave Dad one of her 'are you sure about this?' looks.

Inside, Pepsi raced from one end of the kitchen to the other. Her legs scrambled on the lino each time she turned around.

Jacob babbled in delight and tried to grab the end of her leash. Pepsi raced past him. He spun around, then stumbled and sat on the floor looking a little dazed.

"Pepsi Parsons went past fast." Jacob clapped his hands. Pepsi barked at him.

Mum let out a noisy breath. "That dog is out of control."

"She's a tad excited," Dad said. "They told me this might happen."

Mum gave Dad another special look. "I don't know why I let you talk me into these things, Dave. You'd think I'd remember there's only one responsible adult in this house."

Dad put his arm around Mum and squeezed her tight. "It's because you love me." He gave her cheek a big smooch.

"Ewww." I rolled my eyes. Love stuff is gross.

"The good news," Dad said, "is that the bloke at the pet shelter told me Pepsi is a lovely dog."

Mum raised her eyebrow and didn't say anything.

"Truly." Dad nodded. "He said, and I quote, 'An age-old problem, the boyfriend bought little Pepsi here as a Christmas present, and his girlfriend wasn't impressed. Dogs are forever, not just Christmas. This one's got the potential to be a lovely dog, but right now she's just another unwanted present. Four months after Christmas. That's when we fill up.'"

Mum rubbed her forehead. "Dave, that sounds like a polite way to say she has behavioural problems. At least tell me there's a grace period to return her?"

"Of course, I'm not quite that silly you know."

"What's all the ruckus? Is the new doggie here?" called Granny from the lounge room.

Pepsi stopped her mad dash back and forth on the lino. Her ears pricked up and she bounced into the lounge.

Granny was in her special recliner chair and

had activated the remote control to help her stand up. Pepsi tilted her head to the side and growled softly.

Granny took her hand off the remote, leaving her in a half-sitting and half-standing position. "I don't think she likes the noise."

I nodded and yelled, "I don't think she does either."

I yell at Granny a lot. Not 'cause I'm cross with her, but because she's a little hard of hearing.

I grabbed Pepsi's collar and held on tight. "Try again now."

Granny used the remote to make her chair sit back down while I held Pepsi. She didn't growl this time but her hackles raised.

"I think I'll stay put. I don't want to upset the little doggie on her first day."

I winked at her. "You're a *great* Granny!" I said, and she laughed. That's one of our favourite jokes because Granny is my Mum's Gran, so she really is my Great-granny.

Granny bent forwards and stretched out her hand. "What a nice doggie."

I let Pepsi go so Granny could pat her, but she ignored Granny and leapt onto our sofa. Her front legs went crazy as she started digging.

Mum swatted her rump with a tea towel. "That's enough of that! No digging to China! Besides dog, *you* don't have a passport."

Pepsi gave a short yip and buried her head in the sofa cushions. When she looked up again, her eyes were rolling in the back of her head, and her tongue was lolling out.

"Crazy eyes," Dad muttered.

Pepsi took off at full speed. She raced around our coffee table several times and jumped back onto the sofa, then down to race around the coffee table again.

As she ran, her legs bunched together in quick little strides and her tongue swung from side to side. Watching her made me dizzy.

"More like Psycho Chicken." Mum put her head in her hands and breathed in sharply. "I've a strong feeling this behaviour is why she was unwanted."

Pepsi finished one final lap around the lounge

room. She bunched her legs, leapt onto the sofa then nimbly bounced across and perched herself on the arm of Granny's chair.

"What a good doggie," Granny said as she patted Pepsi on the head. "What's your name?"

"It's Pepsi Parsons," I yelled.

"Pepperoni?"

"Pepsi Parsons!" I yelled again.

"Pepperoni, what a funny name for a doggie."

Pepsi gave a sharp yap.

With a loud slurp, she licked Granny from her hand right up her arm, leaving a trail of slobber.

Granny smiled and shook her head. "I didn't need a bath, doggie."

Pepsi Parsons was the most unladylike dog I'd ever seen and she came with extra slobber, but I already loved her.

3.
Loo For Roo

I TROTTED UP and down the backyard with Pepsi Parsons on the leash, tapping her on the rump and calling out, "Loo for Roo!"

It was Jacob's fault. Yesterday he'd kept up a constant cry of "Pepsi Parsons peed!" And even worse, "Pepsi Parsons pooed!" Every time Jacob dobbed on Pepsi, Mum's mood got darker.

While I was busy cleaning up, I heard Mum snapping at Dad. "You said she was house trained. She clearly isn't house trained."

"It's just a hiccup, love. It will sort itself out with time," Dad said.

"This is not what we agreed upon, Dave. Do something about it."

Dad went to the pet shop and came back with the cutest blue dog cushion with little black paw prints all over it. He helped me make a spot for Pepsi in the laundry. We placed her cushion in the corner with an old blanket from the cupboard. I told Dad that next time he goes to the pet store he should get Pepsi a blue blanket to match.

Dad also got a special rope toy (so she doesn't chew our stuff) as well as a big bag of dried kangaroo treats. "The lady at the pet store thought we might need them to help train Pepsi," Dad said.

Mum looked at him and didn't say a word. He spent the rest of the day mumbling rude words as he installed a dog door into the back security door.

Pepsi didn't like sleeping in the laundry. She howled for most of the night. I wanted to go and cuddle her. I offered to sleep in there with her, but Mum said that wouldn't help her learn anything.

It doesn't seem fair, because when Jacob wakes up in the middle of the night, she doesn't send him back to sleep on his own. He gets to climb into the big bed with her and Dad.

I woke up early. But not early enough. When I opened the laundry door, I knew straight away that Pepsi Parsons had pooed. That's when Mum decided I needed to take more responsibility for Pepsi.

"First off, dogs need simple words," she said and patted the chair beside her. I slid onto it and leaned on my elbows with my best 'I'm listening' expression, to show Mum I was taking dog ownership seriously.

"Telling Pepsi to go to the toilet is a lot of words for a dog. Try saying 'loo' instead. Like you would say 'sit' or 'stay'. Make a routine and keep it simple. Walk her on the leash in the backyard until she goes to the loo. Then reward her."

Mum pointed to the bag of dried kangaroo treats. "Keep it simple with the treats too. You could say treat or treatie, but not dried kangaroo. That's too long."

"What about roo?" I asked.

Mum laughed. "Loo for roo? Yes, that should work nicely. I'm going to set up the kitchen timer to remind you when to take her outside."

The timer buzzed every hour and I took Pepsi outside. We walked up and down the backyard as Mum had instructed. Pepsi thought this was a great game. Nearly every time I let her off the leash, she made a run for it back to the hallway right outside my bedroom door, where she made a mess; the sort of mess that makes Jacob squeal, "Pepsi Parsons peed!"

I tapped Pepsi Parsons on her rump, and with a cry of "Loo for Roo!" we were off again on another lap. Suddenly I felt a strange tugging at the leash. I turned around. Pepsi had stopped.

She was going to the toilet.

Outside.

On the grass.

Not in the hallway outside my bedroom door!

I pulled a piece of dried kangaroo treat out of my pocket. "Good girl," I said and held it out to her. Pepsi chomped away then swallowed with a noisy gulp. I bent down to pat her and she pounced on me.

Oof!

I overbalanced and fell backwards on the grass on my bum.

Jacob ran past and yelled, "Pepsi Parsons pounced!"

Pepsi looked up. I didn't want her to pounce on Jacob and knock him over, so I patted my lap. Pepsi pounced on me. I fell backwards, and we rolled around together for a while. That's when

I remembered the pee spot. I hoped I hadn't rolled in it. I tried to sit up but Pepsi wouldn't let me.

She pounced again and the air rushed out of my lungs. Then she climbed on top of me. Her paws balanced on my shoulders and her puppy breath panted in my face. I tried to push her off, but she was like a dead weight.

My nose filled with slobber and I desperately needed to breathe. I pushed my head to the side and gasped for some air. Pepsi continued licking the side of my face.

I could feel her tail wagging faster and faster. My ear felt as if it was full of slobber. As I opened my mouth and breathed in, Pepsi's tongue slid across my teeth and gums. I pursed my lips shut tight and pushed as hard as I could, but I still couldn't make her budge.

"No licking! Dogs have germs!" Mum yelled from the back patio.

Did she seriously think I had a choice? That I wanted Pepsi to lick my teeth clean? Or that I'd choose to have an ear filled with drool?

I raised my hand and tried to wipe Pepsi's slime off my face. Dad loves the original '80s version of *Ghostbusters*, so when Pepsi first slobbered on him he'd cried out in mock despair, "She *slimed* me!" I knew what Dad meant now. I'd been slimed.

"*Pepsi!*" Mum yelled.

Pepsi's tongue continued to swipe, leaving globs of slobber across my face.

Mum yelled again.

Instead of stopping, Pepsi licked faster. I tried to shove her off me. I turned my face to the side again and gasped in some more air.

Mum came striding towards us with the straw broom.

"One!" Mum strode closer. "Two!" The straw broom swished through the air. "Three!" It thwacked against the fence.

Pepsi startled and looked up at Mum. Mum gave Pepsi one of her raised eyebrow looks. Pepsi didn't move.

Mum stamped the broom against the ground and Pepsi swung round to look at her.

"No more licking faces, Pepsi."

Mum stepped towards us and gave the broom a shake.

Pepsi whined, tucked her tail between her legs and scuttled away to hide behind the barbecue.

4. Sit

FLUSHED WITH MY success at toilet training Pepsi, I moved on to teaching her to sit. It soon became obvious that 'sit' meant nothing to Pepsi Parsons.

Or perhaps it meant 'run around', 'chase your tail', 'jump on the sofa, peer through the window and bark at Smokey, the cat from across the road'. Pretty much everything and anything but 'sit'.

I tried saying 'sit' and sitting down myself, but that didn't work. Instead, Pepsi pounced on me. I flopped on the sofa and waited for her to settle.

"She's more entertaining than the TV," Granny said.

Granny loved watching Pepsi. When Jacob ran into the lounge room, Pepsi's eyes rolled back, and she took off again. Barely pausing for her legs to bunch up, she sprang onto the sofa, then pounced on me before springing back down to do more laps around the coffee table.

Every so often she paused and gave a sharp yap as if she was cheering for herself. On her fifth lap, Pepsi knocked the coffee table.

Granny's cup overbalanced and tea sloshed over the table. Pepsi paused, yapped at the teacup and continued.

Mum stormed into the lounge, straw broom in her hand. "That dog needs to settle. This chaos cannot go on."

When Pepsi saw the broom, she halted in mid-flight, and her tail slunk between her legs. She backed away, her belly low as she tried to hide between Granny's chair and the sofa.

"She'd better not chew those power cords," Mum said.

I hurried to get a tea towel to mop up the spilt tea. When I came back, Granny was patting Pepsi as she lapped up the tea. "Good doggie, Popsicle."

I yelled, "Her name is Pepsi Parsons."

"Yes," Granny said. "Good doggie, Popsicle."

"Pepsi Parsons!" I yelled.

Granny smiled at me and gave Pepsi some of her biscuit. Pepsi stood with her front paws balancing on the arm of Granny's chair and gave her a big slurp all the way up her arm. I mopped up the spilt tea, then used the tea towel to mop up Granny.

I thought Pepsi might have calmed down a little, but no. She spun around, leapt on the sofa and pushed her nose through the slats in the blind. Pepsi barked her biggest *go away* bark. She bounded towards the door and pounced, then she jumped back on the sofa. I tried to grab her in a bear hug to hold her still, but she broke away and leapt at the door again.

Before I could blink, Pepsi was back, launching herself onto the sofa. She stuck her nose through the blinds and peeked out. Smokey was sunning himself on our front veranda. Smokey is a midnight black cat with a white tip on his tail.

He belongs to Rachel, who is possibly the most annoying girl at my school. Since kindy, I'm her favourite target. Mum says I must be doing something to upset Rachel, but I'm sure she's just plain mean.

Smokey seemed to know Pepsi couldn't get outside and carried on nonchalantly cleaning himself. Clearly, he was pretending he was too busy to be bothered by Pepsi's frenzied barking.

"Tell that dog to stop," Mum warned, "or I'm coming in there with the broom. One... two..."

I plonked myself on the sofa next to Pepsi and gave her another bear hug. She growled and rumbled. Her muscles tensed and I knew she was about to launch herself at the window.

"Please, Pepsi Parsons," I whispered, "don't make Mum count to broom."

Pepsi stiffened at the word *broom*. Her brown eyes widened, and she promptly cuddled in close to me. When Mum appeared in the doorway, all was quiet and peaceful.

"Mum," I said, "Pepsi doesn't seem to want to do anything I tell her to do." So far, Mum had given good puppy training advice. But I didn't like reminding her that Pepsi still needed training.

"Routine and rewards, remember? Show her. Don't yell 'sit' at her. She doesn't understand. You need to show her, then reward her."

"But how do I show her to sit? I tried sitting down when I called out 'sit'. Pepsi thought it was a game and leapt on me."

Mum laughed and gave me a cuddle. "Rosie, you do make me laugh. Pass me one of those treats and I'll show you how to get Pepsi to sit."

Mum waved the roo treat and called out to Pepsi. Pepsi jumped up and bounced over. "See how she keeps her eyes on the treat?"

Mum clicked her fingers and called out, "Sit!" Then she raised her hand. Pepsi's eyes followed the treat upwards, then her head moved. Mum continued to move her hand over the top of Pepsi's head, so the only way Pepsi could keep watching was to sit down.

"Good girl," said Mum and gave her the treat.

Pepsi gobbled it.

Mum handed me the treats. "Your turn. I'm off to wash my hands."

I practised the way she'd shown me and, in no time at all, Pepsi was sitting on command!

I sat on the sofa and smiled. Pepsi snuffled in my lap looking for more roo treats. After a while, she relaxed and rested her head on my thigh. Her breath was hot, and it gently puffed down my leg. It was a great cuddle! I sat there

for a few minutes and patted her head. Maybe, with more training, Pepsi could be a little more ladylike.

I sat there lost in a daydream, Pepsi's hot little breath puffed out down my thigh. As it reached my knee, her breath was starting to cool. I looked down and watched a big trail of drool drip down my thigh onto my knee. Then it trickled through my toes.

She had slimed me again. So much for being ladylike.

"Popsicle, come here." Granny waved a piece of biscuit.

"Pepsi Parsons!" I yelled.

"Yes, she is a good doggie." Granny beamed at Pepsi. Pepsi tilted her head to the side and sniffed the air. Granny waved a biscuit at her, but Pepsi didn't pounce. She seemed to sense that Granny was fragile.

Granny held her arm out further, and Pepsi followed, her body swinging around so her gaze never left the biscuit.

"I taught all my dogs like this," Granny said.

She moved her hand backwards over Pepsi's head, and Pepsi Parsons plonked her bottom right down on Granny's foot.

"Ooff, she's weighty," sighed Granny. She looked with dismay at the slobber on her hand.

5.
Thunderstorm

PEPSI WOKE ME when she pounced and landed firmly on my legs. If I'd known she was going to play games, I might not have sneaked her into my room!

I struggled out from under Pepsi and my blankets. Her hackles had risen. She grumbled and muttered, pacing the bed. I listened carefully, but all I could hear was our gate banging in the wind.

A loud boom of thunder broke the silence. Pepsi pounced at the end of the bed and barked at the ceiling.

"Pepsi, shhh!" I grabbed her collar. "It's only thunder."

Lightning flashed, lighting up my bedroom for a few seconds. Another clap of thunder rumbled and roared. Pepsi broke away from my grasp and barked frantically at the ceiling.

Jacob squealed and his footsteps thumped on our floorboards as he ran into Mum and Dad's room. That sent Pepsi into a new frenzy.

I didn't want Mum to catch Pepsi in my room so I put my Smurf slippers on and grabbed Pepsi's collar. We walked quietly towards the back door. Pepsi grumbled a few times, but she didn't try to run away from me. Once outside, I let go of her and pointed to the sky.

"See, Pepsi? No one is out here or on our roof. That's thunder, not a burglar."

Another clap of thunder boomed. Pepsi barked her biggest *go away* bark. Distant rumblings sent her streaking down the side of our house. I padded after her, my nightie flapping around my ankles. I wondered if Pepsi thought she could frighten the thunder away.

Pepsi finished her lap down the side of the house and ran back past me. I turned and chased after her, hoping I wouldn't trip over something in the dark. Jacob has a bad habit of leaving his toys lying around.

A lightning flash lit up our backyard.

Oh no! The gate!

I ran faster, but I was too late. I was just in time to see Pepsi's tail leaving our yard as the light faded.

I raced to the back door and tried to grab

Pepsi's leash. It wasn't there. I started to panic. I hadn't put it away and now I couldn't find it. Another flash of lightning lit up the backyard and I spied Pepsi's leash lying on the table. I snatched it and ran through the gate after Pepsi.

I raced past my bedroom window, past Mum's car and then down our driveway. Thunder boomed, and I jumped. Then Pepsi barked.

I yelled, "Pepsi Parsons!"

At the end of our driveway, I looked both ways, but I couldn't see her. My heart raced.

Where was she?

What if she never came back?

What if I couldn't find her?

What if I lost her?

Something moved across Mrs Winter's front lawn. I hitched up my nightie and ran down the middle of the road. At the corner, I slowed to a walk and carefully made my way up Mrs Winter's driveway.

The thunder boomed, and Pepsi barked another frantic *go away* bark. She ran straight past me. I spun around, nearly stumbling when

I caught my heel on the hem of my nightie.

As the next flash of lightning lit up our street, I saw her race back towards our house. I trotted after her. My heart was beating so fast my chest felt as though it would explode.

Thunder boomed and lightning sparked. The storm was right overhead. Rain started to fall in big heavy drops. From out of nowhere, Pepsi dashed past me. She pranced and pounced in the rain, jumping and trying to catch raindrops.

I leapt towards her, but my feet tangled in my nightie and I tumbled over. Pepsi came to snuffle my face, but when I sat up, she backed away. As the next bolt of lightning blazed, Pepsi pounced towards the road.

She threw something up in the air, then caught it again. As the darkness settled, Pepsi continued her game of catch. I couldn't quite see what she was tossing into the air until she was a little closer.

It was one of my Smurf slippers.

"Bring it here, Pepsi," I called. She kept playing catch with herself, but each time she moved a

little closer. I laughed and held out my hand. Pepsi dropped my slipper, then darted away. It looked as if she knew how to fetch, even if she did do it in a strange way. Maybe we could play catch soon? With a ball next time!

My slipper was soggy. I couldn't tell if it was the rain or Pepsi slobber. I shrugged and put it on anyway. I was getting used to having soggy things.

I stood up and looked around, but I couldn't see Pepsi. My nightie was soaked and clung to me. Pepsi darted past in the dark. Relief flooded through me only to be replaced by panic as I realised she was heading straight towards Rachel's house.

If Smokey was outside how would I stop them from fighting?

Darkness settled, and I could just make out Pepsi snuffling at Rachel's front door. Something had caught her attention.

She pounced towards a dark shadow.

6.
More Trouble

HEART THUMPING, I ran across the road. I'd never seen a dog and cat fight before, but I knew it was trouble.

What if Smokey's claws made a mess of Pepsi's face?

Or if Pepsi bit Smokey?

I couldn't see Smokey anywhere. Pepsi was alone. My heart slowed a little. Pepsi put her head up and yapped as I approached. She no longer seemed concerned about the thunder.

Her tail wagged and she put her head down. I came alongside her and peered into the darkness. Pepsi had found Smokey's food bowl and was busy devouring his cat kibble.

I grabbed Pepsi's collar and clipped her leash on. I hauled her away from Smokey's bowl. I made about five steps before Pepsi dragged me back. She snatched another mouthful. Her tail wagged as she munched.

"Pepsi," I hissed, "we have to go before someone sees us."

Pepsi ignored me and swiped mouthful after mouthful. I hauled on her leash again. This time,

I dug my heels in and pulled with everything I had. Pepsi didn't budge.

Thunder rumbled, sounding further away now. Pepsi lifted her head briefly from Smokey's bowl. Her hackles rose, and she gave a little growl before snatching yet another mouthful.

I tugged and tugged, but couldn't move her. I wasn't about to give up. There must be a reason why dogs and cats have different food. Was it safe for dogs to eat cat kibble?

Lightning flashed, and lit up the street. Pepsi didn't bother to look up or bark. As the shadows of the night settled around us again, I muttered, "Enough! We have to go!"

Pepsi ignored me and scoffed more food.

I kept a firm grip on her leash and started hopping from foot to foot. I always hop when I'm anxious. All I could do was hope Pepsi would finish soon so I could take her home, before someone saw us and before Mum or Dad realised we were outside.

There was a click and a spotlight shone down on us. I blinked a few times in the bright light.

Rachel's front door swung open and my blood froze. When my eyes managed to focus, I saw Rachel smirking at me. Oh no! My soaked nightie was plastered to me. She'd be able to see right through it to my Smurfette undies. My face burned.

Pepsi kept eating. She finished the last mouthful, licked the bowl clean, looked up and burped. Rachel's mum had joined her in the doorway. Pepsi yapped a thank you for the unexpected feast.

I wished the ground would open up and swallow me.

"I spy a runaway," said Rachel's mum. "I'll help you take her home."

"See you tomorrow, Smurf Girl," Rachel said.

I don't honestly know which was worse. Knowing that Rachel couldn't wait to tell the whole school all about this the next day, or Mum's scowl when we knocked on the front door. She thanked Rachel's mum politely, but the minute the door shut behind us she turned and snapped at me.

"Get that dog locked in the laundry where she belongs. Get yourself out of those wet clothes. Then you have some explaining to do, young lady."

I sniffed and sobbed then gasped out that the side gate was still open. Pepsi and I headed to the laundry. I hugged Pepsi and told her, "I'll take all the blame. I'll tell Mum it was my fault. But you have to try extra hard to be good in case Mum's thinking about sending you away." I think Pepsi listened because she licked my hand before I shut the door.

In my bedroom, I changed, then headed back to the kitchen to wait. Mum was still in the bedroom, but the door was open so I heard every word she said.

"Yes you will, Dave," Mum snapped. "Someone has to get up, shut the gate and clean that dog up. I'm not the one who thought it would be a great idea to get a dog. I didn't want a dog. I said it was going to cause trouble. I said you'd have to help Rosie be responsible. And I meant it. Well, there's trouble. And now *you* need to be responsible."

Dad shambled off to shut the gate, muttering under his breath. Mum strode through the kitchen carrying Jacob. She smoothed his head, and whispered to him; he seemed to nod off again into her shoulder.

Dad shuffled back inside. He looked bleary-eyed at Mum as she returned from Jacob's room.

Mum spun him around and pointed him towards the laundry. "Pepsi's wet and needs to be dried off."

Dad nodded and headed for the laundry with a zombie-like shuffle.

Mum stood with her hands on her hips and glared at me. "Start speaking, young lady."

I sniffed and tried to speak but instead of words, silly sounds came out of my mouth. Mum reached for a tissue and waved it towards me. "Blow your nose and try again."

I blew my nose and took a few hiccupping breaths. I left out the part about Pepsi sleeping on my bed and explained that Pepsi had woken me. Then I went through the whole story until

I got to the bit about how Pepsi had pigged out on the cat kibble. As I talked, Mum pulled out a chair and sat down at the table with her face in her hands. She rubbed her temples and sighed a few times.

"Do I even need to tell you how silly you've been?" Mum's voice was very calm.

I sniffed and shook my head.

"Grounded for starters. That dog is truly starting to test my patience."

"Will Pepsi be okay? She ate a lot of cat kibble."

Mum tapped her fingers on the table. "Well, if she ends up with a bellyache she only has herself to blame. It's late. You have school tomorrow. We can discuss this later."

She waved me off, and I crept back to my bedroom. I didn't get straight into bed. Instead, I hovered at the door and listened until Dad finished up with Pepsi. I heard him shuffle back into the kitchen.

Mum's voice snapped like thunder. "I told you, Dave. I told you this dog was a bad choice. But did you listen? 'She needs to settle in', you said.

Look how much trouble she's caused in just one week. It's time to start thinking about taking her back."

Their bedroom door slammed shut. I crept silently into bed. Tears poured down my face.

What if Mum made Dad take Pepsi back to the pet shelter? What would happen to her if she was unwanted twice?

7.
Pepsi Parsons vs the Herb Garden

AS SOON AS the last bell of the day chimed, I raced out of the classroom.

Rachel called out, "Off to steal more cat food?" I swung my bag onto my back and ignored her. It was surprisingly easy to do. Not that I planned on telling Mum that. She'd point out that's the advice she's been giving me along. The truth is, I was too worried about Pepsi to care what Rachel thought. I was sure dogs weren't supposed to eat cat kibble, but I didn't know why.

Mum's car wasn't in the driveway and Pepsi wasn't at the door to meet me.

Something *was* wrong!

Could Mum have taken her away without letting me say goodbye?

I burst into the lounge room. "Where's Pepsi Parsons?" I yelled at Granny.

"They've taken the nice doggie to the vet." Granny patted the arm of her chair. "Come sit down with me."

Shaking, I threw down my school bag. People only asked you to sit down if they had bad news. Had the cat kibble given Pepsi more than a bellyache?

"We were sitting in the garden having a cup of tea. Petunia had a bone. She's such a nice doggie that one. She took off around the corner to eat it," Granny said.

"But instead, she must have decided to bury it. Dogs like to bury their bones. So she dug a hole. Dogs like doing that too you know." Granny patted my arm.

"The problem was, you see, that hole she dug, it was right underneath your mum's herb garden stand. And she dug such a big hole that the whole thing came crashing down. My goodness, it made me jump. I couldn't believe the noise. I thought something had landed on the roof."

My eyes nearly popped out of their sockets. "Did Pepsi get squashed?"

A tiny fluttering feeling of fear radiated from my belly.

"No." Granny shook her head. "But all the pots smashed. Such a shame. Your mum doesn't think she can save any of the plants. Your poor mum, she was cross. That big flowerpot survived. I'm sure that one's indestructible, and it does have a lovely bunch of pansies in that pot."

"But what about Pepsi Parsons?" I cried.

Granny paused to take a sip of her tea then carried on with her story. "Your mum yelled for a bit. Then she got on with cleaning up.

It's so frustrating to be old. All I could do was sit and watch her. I never thought I would end up this lazy you know. Petunia, she's a clever dog. She knew she'd upset your mum. She came over and sat next to my chair while your mum swept up all the mess and put it into garbage bags."

"She's frightened of the broom. Pepsi and the broom are not friends." I made sure I yelled Pepsi's name very clearly so Granny would hear it.

Granny winked at me and continued. "It wasn't until the mess was all cleaned up that your mum noticed Petunia was bleeding."

"Bleeding! And no one noticed?"

"Not much, a little. One of the ceramic pots must have cut her leg when it smashed. Your mum thought it would need stitches. So off they went to the vet. I tell you it was a rather exciting day."

I didn't think Pepsi having to get stitches was exciting, but I heard the rumble of the car in the driveway so I raced outside. Mum opened the rear door, and Pepsi tried to get down from the back seat. She had a plastic cone around her head, which she kept bashing into the side of the car.

Mum carefully lifted her down and handed her leash to me. "Take her inside will you, Rosie?"

She reached over the back seat to help Jacob out of his car seat.

"Three stitches," Jacob said, as he held up four fingers.

I looked in horror at Pepsi's leg. The hair at the top of her left leg had been shaved off, and there were three neat stitches.

As I walked Pepsi towards the front door, she walked sideways and nearly fell. "Mum, she's walking funny!" I cried.

"It's from the anaesthetic," Mum said. "She'll

be a little off balance for an hour or so."

"What's that thing on her head for?" I asked.

"It's an Elizabethan Collar, I've always called it a bucket. It's to stop her nibbling her stitches."

Pepsi slowly followed me into the house. Her bucket banged into my legs at every step. It wasn't long before my heels were a mess of scrapes.

Straight away Pepsi got stuck under the kitchen table.

"Trapped!" Jacob squealed. He started to crawl after her.

I had to pull out the kitchen chairs for her to escape.

"She doesn't have any spatial awareness with that bucket on her head," Mum said.

I'm not sure Pepsi had a lot of spatial awareness *before* she had a bucket on her head, but I'm not one to argue. Instead, I took Pepsi outside and we sat on the grass.

I gave her a cuddle. She got excited and tried to lick me. She couldn't reach, and the bucket banged into me.

At least with the bucket Pepsi couldn't slobber on me. She smashed her bucket into me again and I changed my mind.

Perhaps being slobbered on wasn't so bad after all!

8.
Pepsi Parsons, Flowerpot Puppy

THE WEEK PASSED slowly. Although Pepsi's bucket was plastic, with fifteen kilos of puppy pushing it, it hurt every time she banged into me. I had bruises on both my arms and the back of my legs. My heels were the worst. Dad laughed and said I looked like I'd been in the wars.

I couldn't wait to play with Pepsi properly; I was over being bucket bashed. When the day came to take her to the vet to have the stitches out I wanted to go straight after school, but Mum said, "Later," and shooed me outside.

While we waited, Pepsi and I played fetch. I watched Pepsi scoop her bucket along the grass and flick the tennis ball into the air. She caught it and raced back to me. She skidded to a halt and dropped the ball into my lap. She bent to lick me and her bucket bashed into my arm. I'm pretty sure my bruises had bruises.

I threw the ball, and Pepsi bounced off to chase it. Occasionally she was clever and managed to catch it. Other times she had to keep flicking it along using her bucket like a big shovel.

She ran over to her water bowl and put her

face down to drink, her bucket scraping against the ground. She bounced back towards me and flecks of water and slobber sprayed all over me, right before her bucket bashed into me again.

Pepsi left her ball behind and raced off chasing a butterfly. I lay back on the grass and watched the clouds. I love cloud watching. Sometimes you can see a shape right there in the sky. Sometimes you have to use your imagination a little.

Eventually the patio door swung open and Mum and Jacob came out.

"Time to go and get those stitches out."

Mum stood with her hands on her hips while I sprang to my feet and headed off down the side of the house after Pepsi.

Mum hadn't replaced any of her pots or plants yet so it looked very bare, just a few shrubs and one lonely flowerpot.

When I turned the corner, I could see Pepsi was sitting in the flowerpot. Little pansies sprang out from near her feet and with the bucket on her head she looked like a big flower puppy.

Jacob came running around the side. He saw

Pepsi, laughed and ran back to Mum. "Pepsi Parsons, pansy," he squealed.

I heard Mum coming and hoped Pepsi would stay still long enough for her to see my incredibly cute flower puppy. Mum only ever noticed Pepsi being naughty, and I wanted her to see Pepsi as I did. Cute and fun.

Mum, however, arrived just in time to see Pepsi spring down from the flower pot and her pansies not quite spring back to where they had been before.

I didn't need to turn around to know I was getting one of Mum's looks. Pepsi Parsons slunk past Mum and ran off to sit by Jacob. I turned around to face Mum.

"Mum," I said, "Pepsi has been good all this week."

Mum frowned and rubbed her temples. "Rosie, it's not enough to be good sometimes. I don't think this is working."

My eyes filled with tears and Mum gave me a hug. "I know how much you've always wanted a dog, but Pepsi may not be the right dog for our family. That doesn't mean we won't try again with another dog."

"But I love Pepsi. I don't want another dog." Tears streamed down my face.

Mum hugged me harder, but she didn't say anything else.

9.
Bath Time

PEPSI WRIGGLED AND squirmed while the vet looked at her leg. Both Mum and I had to hold her down. The vet snipped Pepsi's stitches, and we let her go.

She bounced all over the room and gave everyone big kisses. She slurped the treats the vet held out for her.

"She's very active," Mum said.

The vet grinned.

"Working dogs, like blue heelers, need a lot of exercise, and you need to keep their minds engaged. Have you tried a treat ball?"

Mum shook her head.

"The inside is like a maze and when the dog plays with it, a treat rolls through the maze and eventually pops out."

"And how big should we expect her to get?" Mum asked.

The vet did some measurements while Pepsi tried to kiss him. He went back to the computer and frowned. "She's already bigger than the average full-grown female. You said she was eight months old?"

Mum nodded. "Yes, the pet shelter gave us her original papers and vaccination records."

"Well," the vet said, "her feet are quite big and she is still growing. At this rate, I'd say she'll end up a little taller than the average male blue heeler."

Mum wasn't smiling and didn't look at all happy when she paid the bill.

Pepsi sat on the back seat with me.

"Wind your windows down," Mum said. "She stinks. I didn't notice quite how much until we had to get so close to her. She'll need a bath when we get home."

When we got there, Pepsi jumped straight out of the car and trotted to the front door. Jacob, who had been reading with Granny, jumped and squealed with delight when he saw Pepsi without her bucket.

"I'll just get you a cup of tea, Gran. Then Rosie and I will wash that stinky dog." Mum bustled off, and I grabbed Jacob's hand.

"C'mon, I'm going to bath my mucky puppy. Will you help me?"

Jacob clapped his hands and followed me to the bathroom. I put the bath plug in and added some bubble bath. I did the taps because Jacob isn't allowed to touch them yet. He sorted through his toys and chose two rubber ducks for Pepsi.

Mum came into the bathroom. She looked at the bathtub with the bubbles and the two rubber ducks and laughed. She squeezed us both in a big hug. "This looks fabulous, but we're going to wash Pepsi outside."

Jacob snatched up one of his rubber ducks and we all trooped outside. Mum had a bucket full of soapy water sitting next to the hose. Pepsi sniffed it.

"You're going to have to hold her tight, Rosie," Mum warned me.

She turned on the hose. Pepsi tried to catch the water spurting out of it. Pretty soon, I was as wet as Pepsi. Mum turned off the hose and started washing Pepsi with the soapy water. Jacob squeezed his rubber duck.

Pepsi pricked her ears. Jacob squeezed it again under her nose. Pepsi licked the duck.

"That's a good idea, Jacob, keep her amused while I wash her tummy," Mum said.

Jacob offered Pepsi the duck. She carefully took it from his hand. The duck squeaked. Pepsi danced on the spot. She squeaked the duck again. She gave a little quiver, then shook like a wild thing.

Water and bubbles flew everywhere. Even Mum and Jacob got soaked this time. Pepsi squeaked the duck again. She pranced about and shook once more. This time, I couldn't keep my grip on her collar, and she pranced away from me.

"Grab her," Mum yelled.

I leapt towards Pepsi. Every time she took a step the duck squeaked. It sounded as if Pepsi was laughing at us. She raced around the backyard. Droplets of water trailed behind her. Before I could blink, she ran through her dog door and disappeared into the house.

"Don't just stand there," Mum roared. "Get her back outside."

Pepsi stood in the back room. She shook herself and water flew all over the carpet. She

squeaked the rubber duck twice then bounced through to the kitchen.

Her legs scrabbled, and she seemed to run on the spot for a few seconds. I nearly caught her, but she took off again. When she reached the lounge room, Pepsi started dashing around the coffee table.

Granny held onto her teacup. Jacob went one way, and I went the other. Pepsi dashed between us.

The rubber duck was still squeaking but instead of a laughing happy duck, it whined. I heard a thump in the kitchen. I dashed to the doorway and poked my head around the corner.

Uh oh.

Mum had slipped on Pepsi's water trail. She was getting to her feet and didn't look happy!

I turned around and made a last-minute dive across the room to tackle Pepsi. I grabbed at her but she slipped through my hands. Mum stood in the doorway stamping her broom. Pepsi backed right into the corner and slid between the lamp and the sofa.

Mum stamped the broom again. The lamp started to rock. Pepsi burst out, the lamp flipped sideways and fell to the floor.

Mum moved into the lounge shouting and Pepsi hurtled past her, through the house and out of her dog door. When I made it outside, Pepsi was rolling around on the grass. She saw me, sprang up and raced around the yard again.

I followed her down the side and finally managed to trap her in the corner. Mum said nothing when I brought Pepsi back to the tap. She turned the hose on Pepsi and rinsed her off.

"Make sure she's dry, then lock her in the laundry where she can't do any more damage."

I did what she asked and silently helped Mum clean up. Pepsi scratched at the laundry door and whined the whole time.

Dad got home as we finished mopping the kitchen floor.

"Bit of a circus today was it?" he asked.

Mum glared at him. "I've had it up to my eyeballs. I'm done. I've given that destructive menace more than a fair chance. The vet says she hasn't finished growing. If we can't control her now, what's she going to be like in a few months?"

They disappeared into the study. I lurked in the hallway so I could listen. Somehow Dad managed to persuade Mum to postpone a decision until the weekend so it wasn't a *spur of the moment* thing. Did that mean Dad was on my side – or should that be Pepsi's side?

I wasn't sure.

10.
Training Time!

A BIG 'D' was marked on the calendar for next Saturday.

Decision time.

Did Pepsi have a future in our family?

Every time I looked at that 'D', I couldn't stop thinking about all the things Pepsi could do to cause trouble.

Thinking gave me a thumping headache. That's when I realised what I had to do. I had to start dog training seriously.

Pepsi was going to be the best-behaved dog ever!

I started with getting her to shake hands. Great success! It was easy. Pepsi seemed to think it was a great idea. Except sometimes she'd shake hands followed by a big slurp across my face. Would Pepsi being able to shake hands change Mum's mind? It didn't seem useful, more like a good game.

What could Pepsi do that would be helpful to Mum?

I was playing fetch in the backyard with Pepsi when I came up with my best idea. Instead of bringing the ball straight back, Pepsi liked to throw it up in the air and play catch with herself.

Mum's always complaining that everyone leaves their dirty laundry all over the house. I could train Pepsi to take dirty washing to the laundry!

I started with my socks. I threw a sock in the air and Pepsi caught it. She tossed it high up in the air ready to catch it again. Except she didn't always catch it, sometimes she let the sock fall to the floor so she could pounce on it. Pepsi loved this new game.

Each time we'd get a little closer to the laundry. At the laundry basket, I told her in a firm voice to drop it.

She did!

"Good girl," I said and gave her a kangaroo treat. We raced back to my room and started again with my other sock. Pepsi got the hang of it quickly.

Next, we went into Jacob's room and did his socks too.

After school on Wednesday, Pepsi took a sock from the laundry and brought it to me.

She wanted a kangaroo treat. It was a rush

to get the sock back to the laundry before Mum noticed.

On Thursday when I came home there was a whole bunch of socks in my room. Mum had better not see them! I gathered them up and peeked around all the corners on my way to the laundry.

Near the back room, Mum was leaning on the doorframe watching Pepsi and Jacob. I crept past and dumped the socks in the laundry. On my way back to my room I saw Pepsi and Jacob shaking hands.

Mum murmured in a low voice, "Perhaps there might be potential in that dog yet."

I waited until I was out of her sight before I punched the air.

Yes!

Training Pepsi was working.

On Friday morning before school, I found socks lying all around the house. I was sure stray socks around the house wouldn't help Pepsi, especially now Mum was starting to see the good side of her.

At lunchtime, I looked for dog training books in the library. They were all out, but I did find *The Dog on the Tuckerbox*. It's about a dog that looks a bit like a blue heeler. This dog sat on his master's tuckerbox when he was droving. One day, something bad happened. The drover didn't come back and his dog refused to leave the tuckerbox. It's a sad story. But it didn't tell me how the drover had gotten his dog to stay.

I borrowed it, and when I got home, I read it to Pepsi. She bounced around a bit. I'm not sure she listened properly.

"We're going to practise 'stay'," I said, "but unlike the dog from the story, you don't have to stay forever." I don't think she believed me because I couldn't get her to stay anywhere for more than five seconds.

When I told Dad how hard it was to teach her to stay, he laughed and ruffled my hair. "It's good that you're showing a bit of responsibility," he said. "It might even help sway Mum."

At breakfast on Saturday morning, Mum announced we had things to do. I'd wanted to spend the day with Pepsi, just in case it was her last day, but I thought about what Dad had said last night. I had to prove I was responsible enough for a dog. And that meant I couldn't sulk.

The day seemed to stretch on for the longest time. Our first stop was at a party for Jacob. Mum sat with all the grown-ups, and I helped to supervise the party. Pass the Parcel isn't as much fun when you're the one turning the music on and off.

Jacob was all hyped up after the party. Mum said we still had to take him shoe shopping. He'd had a growth spurt and needed new shoes.

All he wanted to do was get up and run around. Last time we were at the shops, and he kept trying to run away, I'd sat on him to make him stay put. Mum was quiet in the shops that day, but when we got home she had yelled something fierce at me! Apparently, sitting on your brother is not the right thing to do.

I didn't want anything to upset Mum today. Each time Jacob made a run for it, I calmly went after him and brought him back, even the times

I thought about sitting on him. I wheeled the trolley for Mum when we did the food shopping. I didn't complain, not even when Jacob climbed on the back of the trolley and made me push him, too.

I kept reminding myself it was for Pepsi. I had to convince Mum that having Pepsi made me more responsible.

As we loaded the shopping into the car, my worries started again. I knew I'd been super good, but had Pepsi? Had she done anything while we were out that might upset Mum? The best thing to do would be to rush inside and check so I could fix any mess before Mum saw it.

I jumped out as soon as the car pulled up in our driveway and hopped anxiously from one foot to another. "Keys please?" I asked Mum as she was helping Jacob out of his car seat.

Pepsi wasn't at the door to greet us.

A coil of fear ran through my belly. Was Pepsi hiding because she'd done something wrong?

"Nice of you to offer to help, Rosie." Mum brushed past me, her arms full of shopping bags.

The coil of fear in my belly grew stronger. Pepsi was always at the door to greet me. Something was wrong. Could she have escaped again?

I heard an anxious little yap and rushed through the lounge room.

No Granny.

No Pepsi.

Pepsi gave another little yap. I checked the back room and laundry. I looked out the back and through the sliding glass door. Granny wasn't sitting outside.

Pepsi yapped again. I turned to go up the corridor to Granny's room and spied her feet before I saw her.

She was lying on the floor with a blanket draped over her.

11.
Old Duck Down

"GRANNY," I YELLED. "What happened?"

Mum followed me up the corridor and shooed Pepsi away. "Gran," she said. "Are you all right?"

Mum knelt by Granny and felt her forehead.

"It was the darndest thing. I tripped over my own feet. And once I was down there was no getting back up again. I was stuck like a beached whale." Granny patted Mum's arm. "I'm ever so glad to see you, though. I need a bit of help to get up."

"Are you in any pain, Gran?" Mum held Granny's hand tight.

"I'm a bit stiff and sore. I don't think I've broken anything. Except maybe my pride. It's a dreadful thing to get old and be helpless."

Jacob ran into Granny's bedroom. He stopped when he saw Granny on the floor. "Old duck down?" he asked.

"Not now, Jacob." Mum checked Granny over carefully.

"This old duck's just fine, young duck," Granny told him.

Jacob had started calling Granny 'old duck' in

the last week. He'd brought a silly book home from the library about an old and a young duck. He'd made Granny read it to him over and over. Ever since, he'd called Granny 'old duck' and she called him 'young duck'.

It was cute at first.

Mum sat back on her heels, looking relieved. "I don't think anything is broken either, Gran. You do, however, have a nasty bruise just above your elbow."

"I believe I have a matching one on my back. I came down with quite a thump. So careless of me."

"I'm going to help you sit up."

Mum motioned for me to move to the other side of Granny. "I'm going to slip my arm behind Granny's back and lift her and I need you to support her on your side," she said.

Together we helped Granny up to a sitting position. It wasn't as hard as I thought it would be.

"That's better," said Granny. "I just need to find my sea legs, and I'll be off again."

Mum chuckled and folded the blanket. "So long as you take it slowly, Gran. I'm going to get you the rest of the way up now."

She handed me the blanket and stood behind Granny. Granny lifted her arms out and Mum put her arms around her, sort of like a big bear hug from behind.

She hoisted Granny to her feet. Granny was a bit wobbly; she needed to lean on Mum. They shuffled along towards Granny's comfy chair in the corner of her bedroom.

Granny sat down. Her face lit into a big smile. "Now, this is much more pleasant than being on the floor."

Mum grabbed the blanket from me and started to tuck it over Granny's legs. Pepsi jumped up and licked Granny's hand. Mum shooed her away.

Granny put her hand on Mum's arm. "Leave little Peppercorn. She's been great company."

Mum eyed Pepsi suspiciously. "Did you trip or did Pepsi knock you down?"

Granny shook her head. "She wasn't here. But I don't know what I would have done without little Peppercorn. I let out such a yell. I think you'd just left. I could move my arms fine. I just couldn't roll over to get up. Little Peppercorn raced in. She kept me company all day. Gave me quite a wash she did!"

Granny patted Pepsi. "I got cold after a while, and I was shivering. Peppercorn snuggled up to me. I was still cold. I remember telling her I wished I had a blanket. She raced off. I wondered what on earth she was doing. When she came back dragging her blanket, I was ever so pleased to see her. I managed to drape the blanket over myself. Between the blanket and little Peppercorn snuggling up to me, I managed to get nice and toasty."

Mum raised her eyebrow at Pepsi.

"I've been teaching her to fetch," I said. "And to put things away. Except that hasn't worked quite so well and she started taking socks *from* the laundry instead of taking them *to* the laundry."

"Yes." Mum laughed. "I have noticed some unusual sock activity." As she turned back to Gran, her mouth dropped open. "Rosie, fetch

Granny's throw rug. This is Pepsi's blanket. It's covered in dog hair!"

Granny tilted her head on one side, her eyes twinkling. "Well, where else did you think she'd get a blanket, Karen? You didn't think she'd opened the cupboard up and fetched a clean one, did you? Beggars can't be choosers, my dear, and I can tell you I was very glad I had a blanket no matter how hairy it was." She waved her finger at Mum.

Pepsi and Jacob followed me as I went to fetch Granny's rug from her chair in the lounge. As we passed the kitchen, Jacob started quacking like a duck and making flapping noises.

Pepsi thought it was a great game and pranced alongside him. She gave a little yap every so often. I left them and took the rug back to Granny's room.

Mum tucked it snugly around Granny. "That's better." She straightened up, turned to me and smiled. "You've been such a good little helper today, Rosie."

"And Pepsi too," I reminded her. "Pepsi's been

very helpful with Granny today."

"Yes, quite right, Pepsi has indeed been useful today." Mum smoothed Granny's hair. "Is there anything I can get for you, Gran?"

"I'm a bit parched. A cup of tea would go down a treat."

"I'll put the shopping away; then I'll bring you a nice cup of tea. And I think you should stay and talk to Gran for a while, Rosie."

I sat on the edge of Granny's chair. I was telling her about my day when I heard Mum yell, "*Stop that, you dirty dog!*"

I rushed down the corridor in time to see Mum dash out of the kitchen. At the lounge door, she stood with her hands on her hips. I couldn't see past her but I heard Jacob laughing.

Mum took a step into the lounge room, giving me a clear view. Pepsi was prancing around the coffee table, a trail of sausages bouncing along behind her.

Mum was breathing in and out heavily, trying to control her temper.

"*Pepsi!*" she roared.

Pepsi stopped and looked at Mum. She gulped down several sausages. Her eyes never left Mum's face.

"Drop it, Pepsi!" I called.

Pepsi looked at me. I saw the confusion in her eyes. She didn't drop the sausages.

Mum glared at me. "*That* was our dinner, Rosie Parsons."

Pepsi backed up slowly, away from Mum. She turned and darted behind Granny's recliner chair. One sausage caught on the carpet and was left behind. Mum stood still, her hands on her hips.

Pepsi poked

her head out. She looked at the last sausage still sitting on the carpet, and licked her lips. In a flash, Pepsi bounced out, grabbed the sausage and scurried backwards into her hidey-hole.

There was a loud slurp.

Then a burp.

Mum had had enough. "Take that dog outside. I want her out of my sight right now! I do *not* want to see her again tonight."

12.
The Decision

JACOB WAS THE first to meet Dad at the door. He babbled on about 'old duck down'.

Dad was full of concern when Mum told him how we'd found Granny. He laughed the biggest belly laugh ever when she got to the part about the sausages. Jacob laughed too, and Mum got all huffy.

Dad rang up and ordered pizza. He even organised Jacob for bed.

Usually, pizza is a treat, but it didn't feel like that tonight. I couldn't stop thinking about that 'D' on the calendar. I tried hard not to cry.

Granny rubbed my arm. "Things will work out for the best, little Rosie."

Would they?

I didn't know what I was going to say. When Mum started clearing the table, I helped her. Pepsi whined at the back door and Mum scowled.

"Let little Pattycake in, Rosie. She's full of life. I adore watching her," Granny said.

I ran to open the big door so Pepsi could use her dog door again. I didn't want to miss anything.

"For what it's worth, I like the little doggie,"

Granny said as Pepsi raced past me heading straight for the kitchen.

Mum sighed. "The trouble is, Gran, she's not a little doggie. She's already past the average size for a blue heeler. And it looks as if she hasn't quite finished growing yet."

I sat back down at the table. Mum didn't seem as angry as she was before dinner, but she still didn't sound as though she was in a good mood.

"The internet lies," Dad said, and his eyebrows furrowed together. He does that when he's joking.

"Dave, you based your decision on one website and an adorable photo. And yes, as it turns out when we did a little more research, maybe a blue heeler isn't the right sort of dog for us after all. You have something to learn from this too." Mum folded her arms and leant on the table.

"Okay, point taken. The internet lies sometimes. I vow to be more internet savvy in the future." He put his hand on his heart and looked solemnly at Mum.

Mum rolled her eyes at him, then got down to business. "Who wants to speak first then?"

Granny patted Mum's arm. "I'll say my piece dear. I like little Pattycake. She's a little mischievous. Don't forget, she's young yet. I've had dogs all my life, and most of them started out a little rough. This one's got potential. I think little Pattycake should stay. There, I've had my say, and I'll be heading off to bed now."

We all said goodnight to Granny as she stood and shuffled off slowly.

Mum raised her eyebrows. "Who's next then?"

I was all ready to start with a passionate plea, but Dad jumped in. "The facts are, she's trouble, and she's a nuisance. Certainly, in a short space of time she's cost an awful lot of money. Not to mention the sacrilege of eating the sausages."

My eyes widened, and I looked at Dad, horrified. This was not going well. He had just reminded Mum about all the naughty things Pepsi had done. And I'd thought he was on our side!

My heart thumped madly, and I had a mass of butterflies flying around my stomach. Tears pooled in my eyes.

I put my head in my hands. It wouldn't be

helpful if the only thing I could do was sob when it was my turn to speak.

"I may have made a mistake and believed the first website I came across. I may not have looked into the difficulties of having such an active dog," Dad continued.

"That's a bit of an understatement," Mum said.

"I take full responsibility for that. Certainly, if we had looked into things a little more, we probably would have selected a different breed of dog. But we didn't. We chose Pepsi. Now there was at least one thing on that website that was true. It said that blue heelers are loyal dogs. That was one of the things that you and I discussed was important."

Dad jabbed his finger onto the table to make his point. "Today Pepsi chose us. She chose to stay with your Gran. She chose to go and fetch her blanket and share it. She had the run of the house. There are endless things she could have done. Instead, she proved she is loyal. She considers us her family and she will look after and protect us."

Dad waved his hands about. "We cannot repay loyalty like that by evicting her. Pepsi is family. I vote for Pepsi to stay. There will be ups and downs, but we will weather them together as a family. We will..." His voice trailed off.

Mum had raised her index finger for him to stop talking. "Dave," she said, "it's no secret that I was against the idea of having a dog in the first place. If anything, Pepsi embodies everything that I don't like about dogs."

I buried my face in my hands again.

"She has no manners. She's out of control. Her behaviour is embarrassing. She's destructive, and she's been a huge financial burden on this family. Ever since she arrived she's been nothing but an endless bundle of trouble."

My stomach butterflies all took flight together.

"But you're right. Pepsi has proved she is part of the family today. She could have taken advantage of Gran's little spill and destroyed any number of things. She didn't. In a time of crisis, she was well behaved. Although she did revert to form and manage to take advantage of the sausages afterwards."

I took a deep breath and looked up. Did this mean Pepsi could stay?

"Gran's right," Mum said. "She does have the potential to make a loyal, faithful dog. She can stay. On one condition."

Mum held up her index finger again. "Dog training classes. You and Rosie have to take Pepsi to dog training classes. It's quite clear that we need help."

I squealed and jumped up and down. I hugged Mum first and then Dad. Pepsi joined in the excitement and started bouncing around, too.

When I let go of Dad, she bounced at him for a hug too. Dad laughed and gave her a head rub. Pepsi pivoted and pounced at Mum.

Mum pushed her firmly back on the floor in her no-nonsense manner.

"And this," Mum said with a wave of her hand, "is a fine example of why she needs training."

I sat on the floor and let Pepsi Parsons climb into my lap. I wrapped my arms around her and whispered, "You can stay," into her fur.

She looked up at me with her big chocolate brown eyes and gave me a big slurp right across my face.

She slimed me, and I didn't care.

Pepsi Parsons was family.

Meet the real Pepsi Parsons!

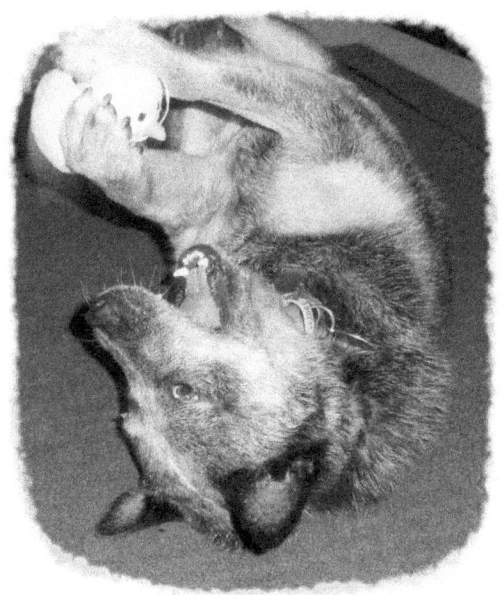

Pepsi Parsons is a disgracefully behaved but sweet-natured Working Dog. Pepsi takes her role of Canine Story Advisor seriously, putting much thought and practice into the antics and shenanigans of her fictional counterpart.

In her spare time, Pepsi enjoys lazing in the sun and volunteers as Chief of Border Security for her household.

www.pepsiparsons.com.au

www.ingramcontent.com/pod-product-compliance
Lightning Source LLC
Chambersburg PA
CBHW052027290426
44112CB00014B/2411